Life is beautiful & pignant —
may you "squeeze out the juice"
with relish.

Roz Halper

The Hands of Life

ALSO BY ROE HALPER

"TO LIFE"
"TEARS OF THE PROPHETS"
"THE CROWN OF LIFE"

The Hands of Life

by Roe Halper

BAYBERRY PRESS   WESTPORT, CONNECTICUT

To my husband Chuck
my son David
my daughter Jan

whose hands have a unique beauty
equal to
the exquisiteness of their souls.

PREFACE

The struggle of humanity—a heavy theme to portray, especially by an artist who has lived a comfortable, secure life full of abundant joy and blessing. So why try such a theme? Because deep within me is this core of empathy for the human being who must summon inner strength to grow, to strive, to build, to create. Such challenges take a power of consequence.

Instead of taking the realistic approach of using the full human figure, I have chosen only the hand—so expressive of mood and emotion. The hand represents a person, and the abstract brush strokes represent the forces of life.

The format is the seven stages of life, yet I have switched "the worker" and "the adult" categories to "the oppressed" and "the fulfilled." And so there is "the child" who is innocent, "the youth" who learns about life and also struggles to break away from controls, "the soldier" who fights for an ideal and fights for his life, "the lover" whose joy balances the tumults of life, "the oppressed" who are the victims of society, "the fulfilled" who are the builders of society, and "the elders" who age either with dignity or despair.

Indeed, there is room for interpretation and perhaps the viewer sees a different message than I. But there is no doubt that I reveal a bittersweet approach to life. Life to me is not to be taken lightly. It is a gift to savor and relish with appetite. There seems so much to do of importance, of contribution, of giving to one's fellow human beings. If there is to be a purpose for this book, it is to illuminate not only the struggle but the poignancy and the exquisiteness of life.

Roe Halper

Westport, Connecticut

The Hands of Life

" Nothing at bottom is real except humanity,"

— Auguste Comte

THE CHILD

"When the voices of children are heard on the
green
And laughing is heard on the hill,
My heart is at rest within my breast
And everything else is still."

— William Blake

"He smiles and clasps his tiny hand,
    With sunbeams o'er him gleaming,—"

— Joseph Ashby-Sterry

" Surprised by joy — impatient as the wind."

— William Wordsworth

" To see a world in a grain of sand
And a heaven in a wild flower
Hold infinity in the palm of your hand
And eternity in an hour. "

— William Blake

"And the song from beginning to end,
I found in the heart of a friend."

— Henry Wadsworth Longfellow

"A rosebud set with little willful thorns"
— *Alfred Lord Tennyson.*

THE YOUTH

"Youth's the season made for joys."
— *John Gay*

"A boy's will is the wind's will
And the thoughts of youth are long,
long thoughts."

— Henry Wadsworth Longfellow

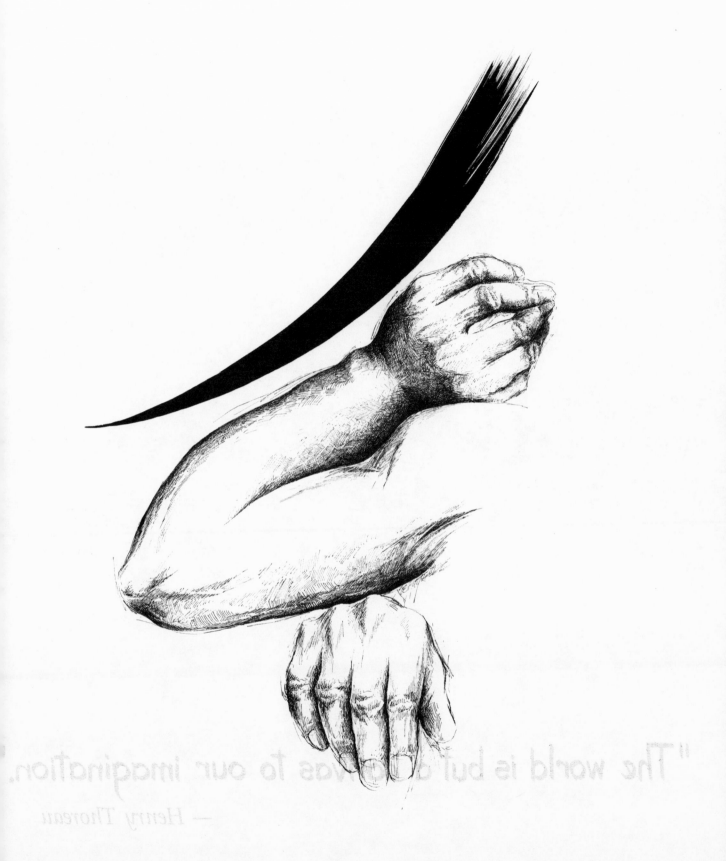

"The world is but a canvas to our imagination.

— Henry Thoreau

"So many worlds, so much to do,
So little done, such things to be."

— *Alfred Lord Tennyson*

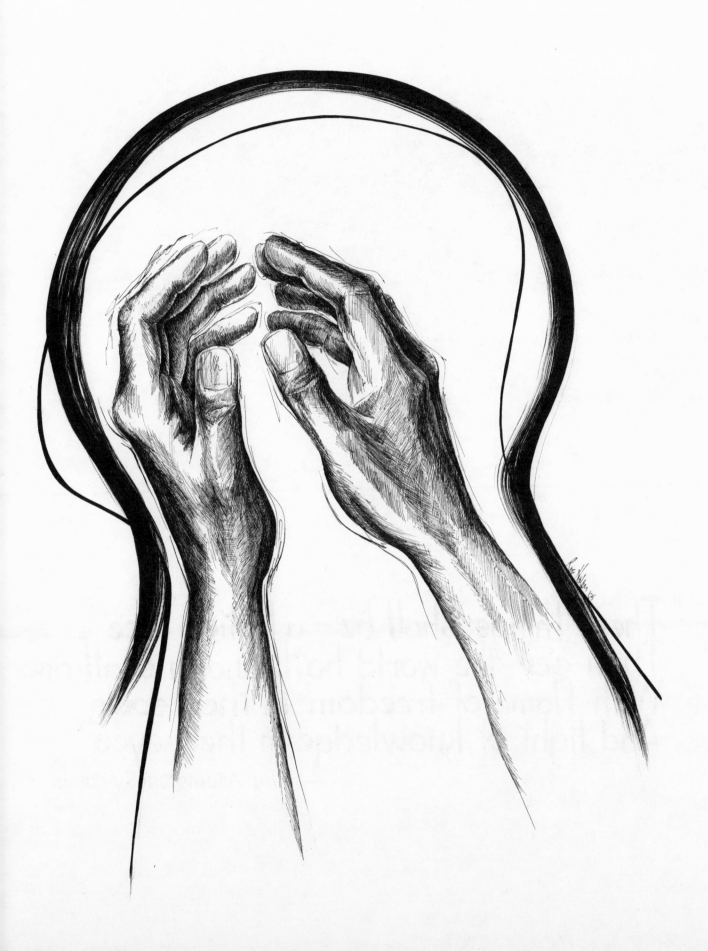

"These things shall be – a loftier race
Than e'er the world hath known shall rise
With flame of freedom in their souls,
And light of knowledge in their eyes."

— John Addington Symonds

"The anchor heaves, the ship swings free,
The sails swell full. To sea, to sea!"

— Thomas Lovell Beddoes

THE SOLDIER

" Let him not boast who puts his armor on,
As he who puts it off, the battle done."

— Henry Wadsworth Longfellow

Fight for life and you will find
    Immeasurable source of strength
To let you give – create anew –
        to fulfill your destiny.

" The bravest battle that ever was fought;
  Shall I tell you where and when?
  On the maps of the world you will find it not;
  It was fought by the mothers of men. "

— Joaquin Miller

" My Triumph lasted till the Drums
Had left the Dead alone
And then I dropped my Victory
And chastened stole along
To where the finished Faces
Conclusion turned on me
And then I hated Glory
And wished myself were They...."

— Emily Dickinson

"He was white and now is red.
Blood has reddened him.
He was red and now is white.
Death has whitened him.

To the right and to the left
In back and in front
The red and the white.
— Mama!"

— *Marina Tsvetaeva*

" Side by side they lie —
All one fate they share,
See how soldiers die,
Where are ours? Where theirs?

— *Marina Tsvetaeva*

THE LOVER

" What is life without the radiance of love ?"
— Johann von Schiller

"The windows of my soul I throw
Wide open to the sun."

— John Greenleaf Whittier

"She smiled, and the shadows departed,
  She shone, and the snows were rain,
And he who was frozen-hearted,
  Bloomed up into love again."

— John Addington Symonds

"How do I love thee? Let me count the ways.
I love thee to the depth and breadth and height
My soul can reach, ... I love thee with the breath
Smiles, tears, of all my life !"

— Elizabeth Barrett Browning

"Love is not love
Which alters when it alteration finds,
Or bends with the remover to remove:
O no! it is an ever-fixed mark,
That looks on tempests and is never shaken;"

— William Shakespeare

" Let those love now who never loved before;
   Let those who always loved, now love the more."

— *Thomas Parnell*

THE OPPRESSED

"Man's inhumanity to man
Makes countless thousands mourn!"

— *Robert Burns*

The 'oppressed' was first conceived as a series on the Holocaust. The bold stroke represents the smokestack of the crematorium. The fist is the symbol of humanity's struggle to rise out of the ashes like a bud thrusting towards light and life.

"Where there is sorrow there is holy ground."

— Oscar Wilde

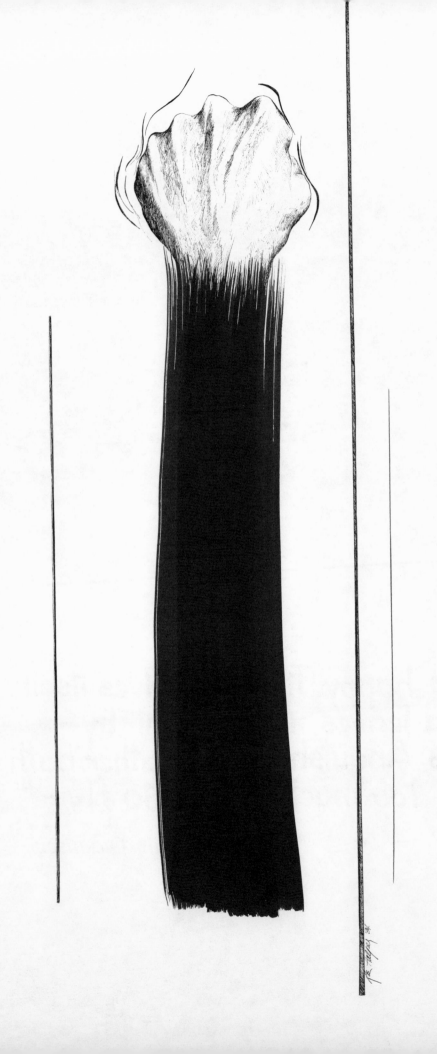

" Too happy Time dissolves itself
And leaves no remnant by –
'Tis Anguish not a Feather hath
Or too much weight to fly – "

— Emily Dickinson

" It might be lonelier
Without the Loneliness –
I'm so accustomed to my Fate –
Perhaps the Other – Peace –

Would interrupt the Dark –
And crowd the little Room –...

I am not used to Hope –
It might intrude upon –
Its sweet parade – blaspheme the place –
Ordained to Suffering –... "

— Emily Dickinson

" Prayer is the soul's sincere desire
    Uttered or unexpressed;
The motion of a hidden fire
    That trembles in the breast. "

— James Montgomery

"A hope beyond a shadow of a dream."

— *John Keats*

"All I care about is life, struggle, intensity."

— Emile Zola

" I know of no more encouraging fact than the unquestionable ability of man to elevate his life by a conscious endeavor..... To affect the quality of the day that is the highest of arts."

— Henry Thoreau

" I find the great thing in this world is not so much where we stand, as in what direction we are moving: To reach the port of heaven, we must sail sometimes with the wind and sometimes against it – but we must sail, and not drift nor lie at anchor."

— *Oliver Wendell Holmes*

THE ELDER

"Old age: the crown of life, our play's last act."

— *Cicero*

"A house of Dreams untold
 That looks out over the whispering treetops
 And faces the setting sun."

— *Edward McDowell*

"Nothing...is more beautiful than the love that has weathered the storms of life...."

— Jerome Klapka Jerome

" The Leaves of Life keep falling one by one. "

— Edward Fitzgerald

"O spare me, that I may recover strength, before I go hence, and be no more."

— *Psalm 39:12-13*

"He has done with roofs and men
Open, Time, and let him pass."

— Louise Imogen Guiney

"Because I could not stop for Death,
He kindly stopped for me –
The Carriage held but just Ourselves
And Immortality."

— Emily Dickinson